American Symbols

The Bald Eagle

By Lloyd G. Douglas

Welcome Books™

Children's Press®
A Division of Scholastic Inc.
New York / Toronto / London / Auckland / Sydney
Mexico City / New Delhi / Hong Kong
Danbury, Connecticut

Photo Credits: Cover, p. 5 © Eyewire; p. 7 © Independence National Historical Park; pp. 9, 21 (top left) © Bettmann/Corbis; pp. 11, 15, 21 (top right) © Digital Stock; p. 13 © Leo Keeler/Animals Animals; pp. 19, 21 (bottom right) © Kevin Fleming/Corbis; Contributing Editor: Jennifer Silate
Book Design: Christopher Logan

Library of Congress Cataloging-in-Publication Data

Douglas, Lloyd G.
    The bald eagle / by Lloyd G. Douglas.
    p. cm. — (American symbols)
    Summary: Describes traits that make the eagle a good symbol for the United States, briefly explains how the eagle was chosen, and lists some of the places the symbol appears.
    Includes bibliographical references and index.
    ISBN 0-516-25851-6 (lib. bdg.) — ISBN 0-516-27874-6 (pbk.)
    1. United States—Seal—Juvenile literature. 2. Bald eagle—United States—Juvenile literature. 3. Emblems, National—United States—Juvenile literature. 4. Animals—Symbolic aspects—Juvenile literature. [1. United States—Seal. 2. Bald eagle. 3. Eagles. 4. Emblems, National. 5. Signs and symbols.] I. Title. II. Series: American Symbols

    CD5610 .D68 2003
    929.9—dc21

                                                    2002152678

Contents

The **bald eagle** is the **national symbol** of America.

It was made the national symbol more than two hundred years ago.

5

Some people did not want the bald eagle to be the national symbol.

Benjamin Franklin wanted the turkey to be the national symbol.

In 1782, the bald eagle was first used in the **Great Seal of the United States**.

9

The bald eagle is a very strong bird.

It stands for America's **strength**.

Bald eagles live for
a long time.

Americans hope that
America will stay strong
for a long time.

The bald eagle flies freely in the sky.

The bald eagle also stands for **freedom** in America.

Today, a picture of the bald eagle is on many things.

It is on American money.

Many buildings in America have **statues** of bald eagles on them.

1819

19

The bald eagle is an important American symbol.

21

New Words

bald eagle (**bawld ee**-guhl) a big bird that has a white head, long wings, and a curved beak

Benjamin Franklin (**ben**-juh-min **frank**-lin) an American leader who lived from 1706 to 1790

freedom (**free**-duhm) being able to go where you want or do what you want

Great Seal of the United States (**grayt seel uv thuh yoo**-nyt-ed **states**) a symbol used on money and other official things

national (**nash**-uh-nuhl) having to do with a nation as a whole

statues (**stach**-ooz) sculptures of people or animals made out of stone, metal, wood, or clay

strength (**strengkth**) being strong

symbol (**sim**-buhl) a drawing or an object that stands for something else

To Find Out More

Books
The American Eagle
by Lynda Sorensen
Rourke Publishing

The American Eagle: The Symbol of America
by Jon Wilson
The Child's World

Web Site
The American Eagle Foundation
http://www.eagles.org
Learn about the bald eagle on this informative Web site.

Index

About the Author

Lloyd G. Douglas is an editor and writer of children's books.

Reading Consultants

Kris Flynn, Coordinator, Small School District Literacy, The San Diego County Office of Education

Shelly Forys, Certified Reading Recovery Specialist, W.J. Zahnow Elementary School, Waterloo, IL

Sue McAdams, Former President of the North Texas Reading Council of the IRA, and Early Literacy Consultant, Dallas, TX